For the A in my alphabet

This is an Arthur A. Levine book
Published by Levine Querido

LQ
LEVINE QUERIDO

www.levinequerido.com · info@levinequerido.com
Levine Querido is distributed by Chronicle Books, LLC
Text and illustrations copyright © 2022 by Ellen Heck

Library of Congress Cataloging-in-Publication data is available
ISBN 978-1-64614-127-2
Printed and bound in China

MIX
Paper from
responsible sources
FSC™ C104723

Published in April 2022
First Printing
Book design by Jon Gray, Ellen Heck, and Semadar Megged
The text type was set in Caslon. Hand lettering by Jon Gray.
The art for this book was created on scratchboard.
The panels were scanned and enlarged to show texture,
then digitally colored and arranged.

A

Is for

BEE

an alphabet book
in translation

Ellen Heck

LQ
LEVINE QUERIDO

MONTCLAIR · AMSTERDAM · HOBOKEN

We speak to each other in many languages,
and in some of them . . .

Biri
in
Hausa

Bandar
in
Hindi

Bojog
in
Balinese

Bеždžionė
in
Lithuanian

B IS FOR Monkey

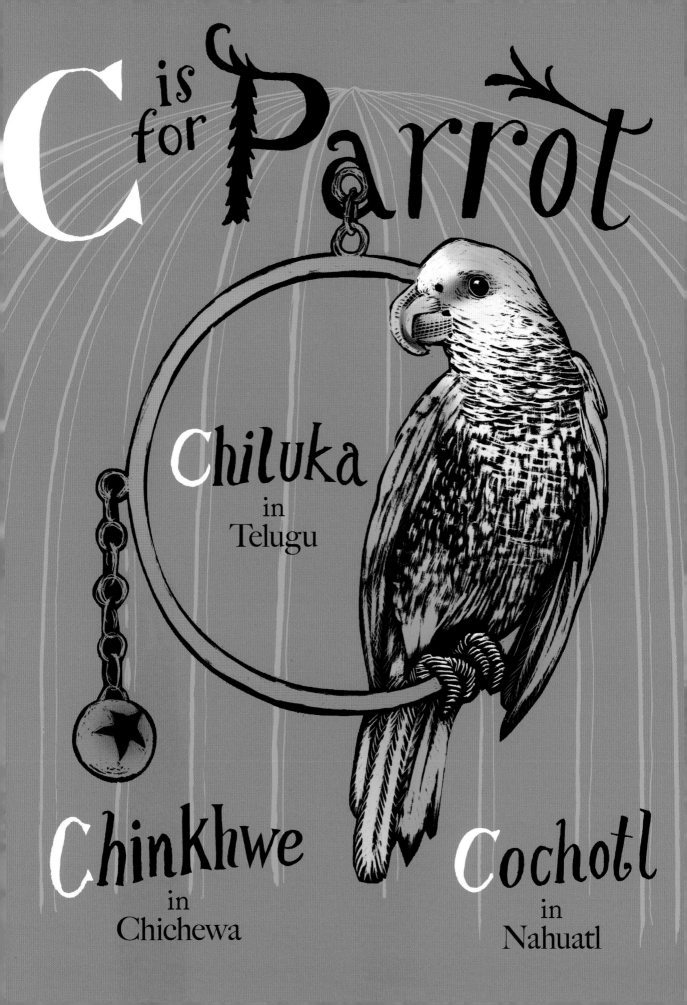

C is for Parrot

Chiluka
in
Telugu

Chinkhwe
in
Chichewa

Cochotl
in
Nahuatl

D is for Turtle

Daksi
in
Cherokee

Dortoka
in
Basque

Deckelsmouk
in
Luxembourgish

Dtào
in
Thai

Etmaewig
in Chechen

Escargot
in French

Etana
in Finnish

E is for Snail

Elagwa
in Cherokee

F is for Butterfly

Flutur
in
Albanian

Farasha
in
Arabic

Farfalla
in
Italian

Féileacán
in
Irish

Gato
in
Spanish

Gaazhagens
in
Ojibwe

Goyangi
in
Korean

G is for Cat

H is for tiger

Huli
in
Kannada

Harimau
in
Indonesian

Inhlanzi in Zulu

Ikan in Malay

Iqalluk in Alutiiq

I is for fish

Iwak in Javanese

Isda in Tagalog

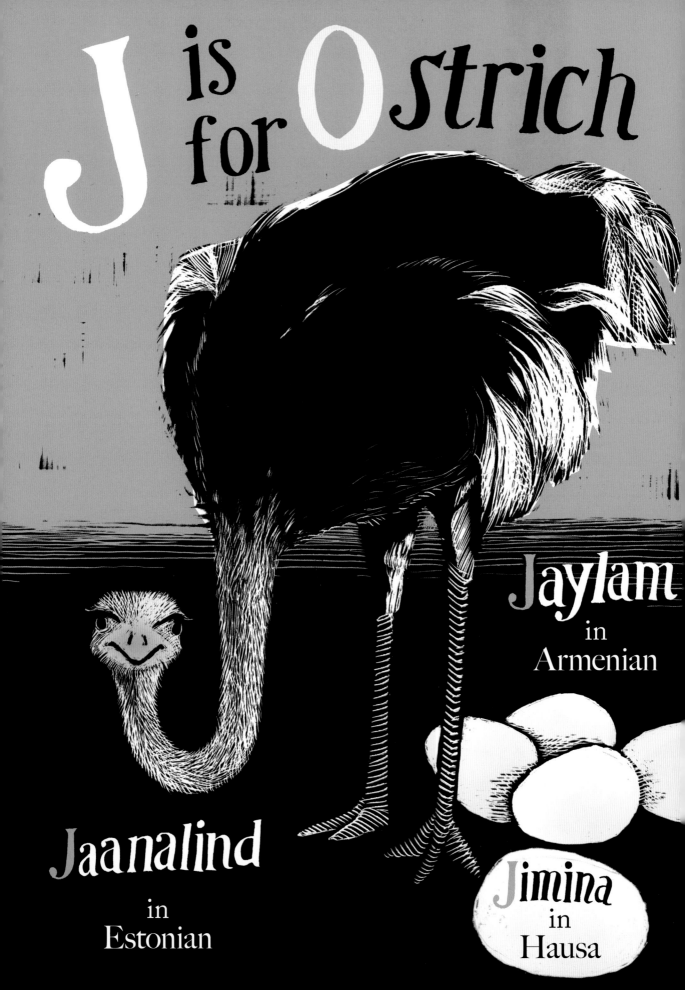

J is for Ostrich

Jaylam
in
Armenian

Jaanalind
in
Estonian

Jimina
in
Hausa

Kakīroa in Māori

Kirahvi in Finnish

K is for giraffe

Kaelkirjak in Estonian

Kamilopárdali in Greek

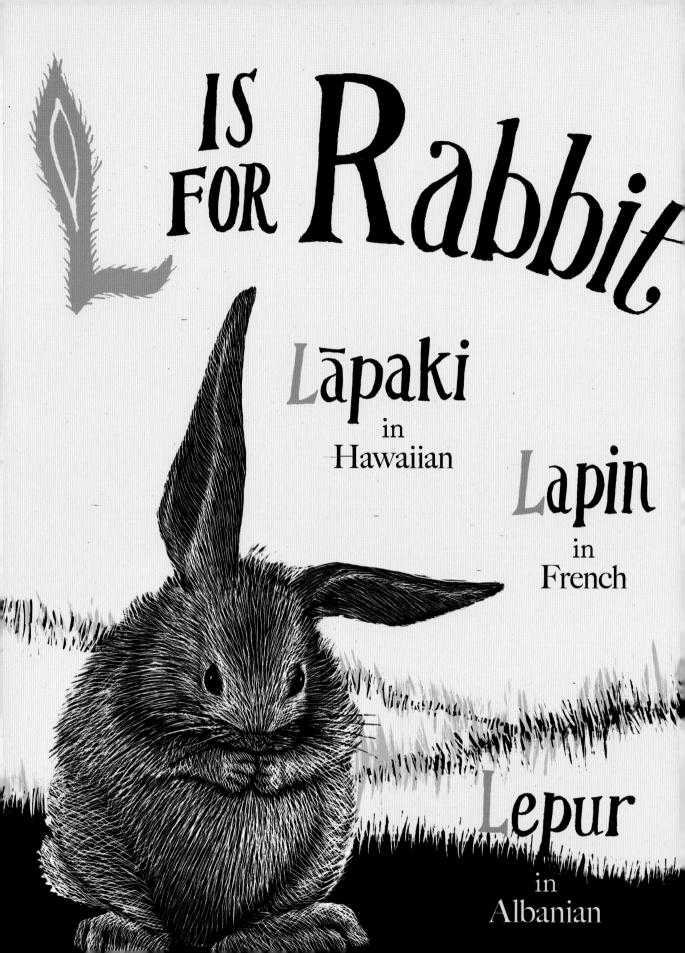

L IS FOR Rabbit

Lāpaki
in
Hawaiian

Lapin
in
French

Lepur
in
Albanian

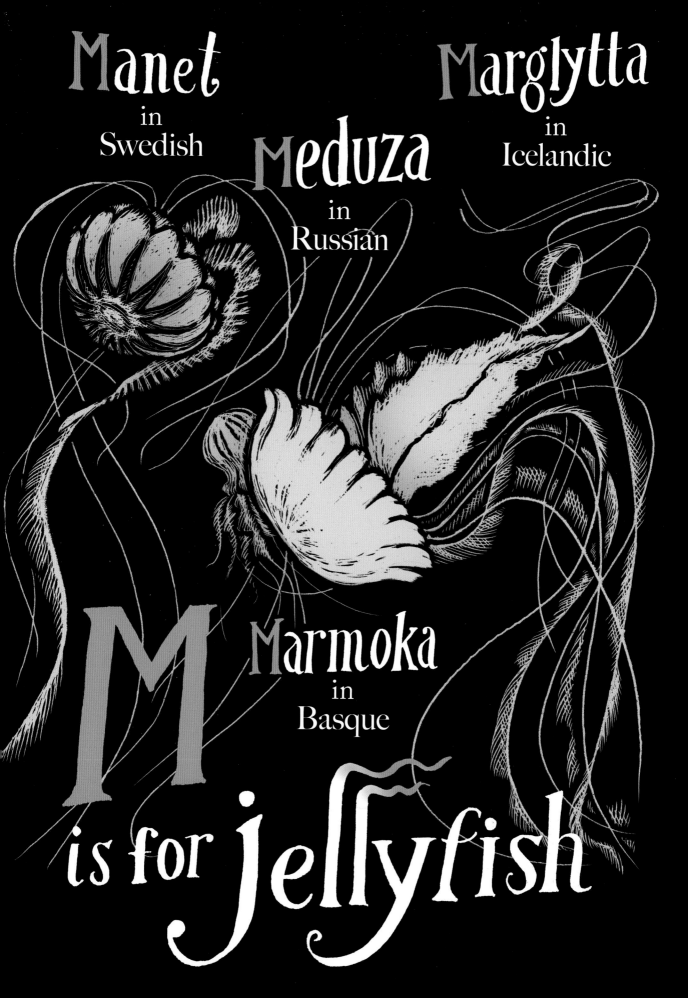

Manet
in
Swedish

Meduza
in
Russian

Marglytta
in
Icelandic

M Marmoka
in
Basque

is for jellyfish

N IS FOR Sloth

Namuneulbo
in
Korean

Ndilna'ii
in
Navajo

Namakemono
in
Japanese

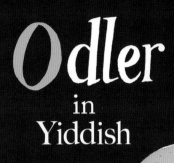**O**dler
in
Yiddish

**O**rzeł
in
Polish

Orel
in
Ukrainian

**O** is for **Eagle**

Q is for frog

Qīngwā
in
Mandarin

Qurbağa
in
Azerbaijani

R IS FOR fOX

Ræv
in
Danish

Rovî
in
Kurdish

Renard
in
French

Róka
in
Hungarian

Rubâh
in
Persian

T is for Octopus

*T*ako
in
Japanese

*T*manun
in
Hebrew

*T*intenfisch
in
German

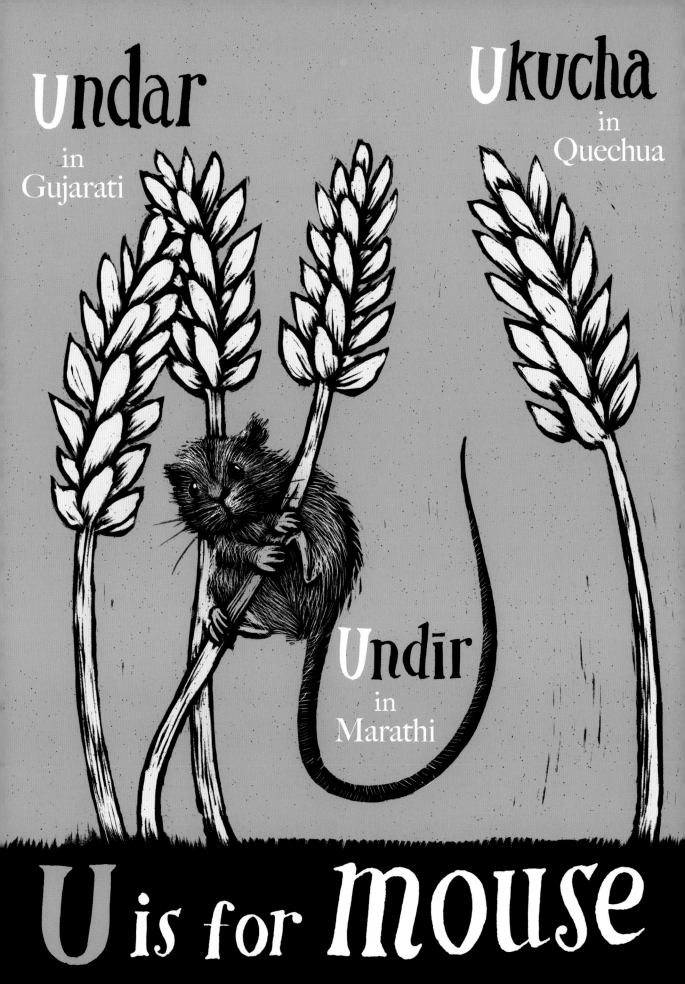

Undar
in
Gujarati

Ukucha
in
Quechua

Undīr
in
Marathi

U is for Mouse

V is for Zebra

Varikkutirai in Tamil

Wahid Alqarn
in
Arabic

Wànga-lànga
in
Wolof

Wiyil
in
Somali

W is for rhinoceros

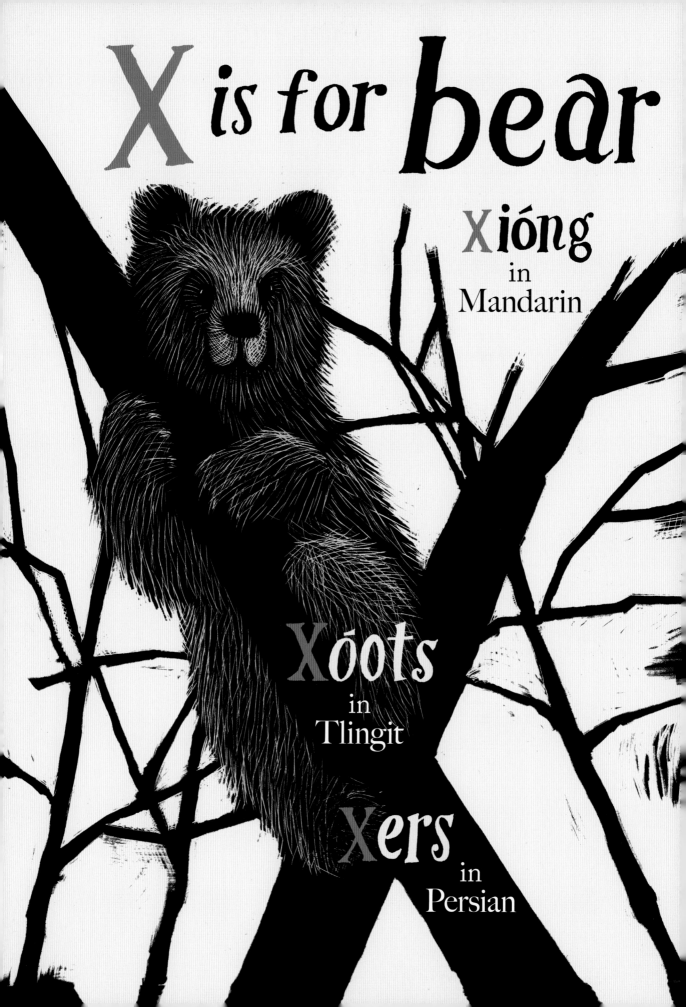

X is for bear

Xióng
in
Mandarin

Xóots
in
Tlingit

Xers
in
Persian

Y is for porcupine

Yamaarashi
in
Japanese

Ystervark
in
Afrikaans

Z is for elephant

zaan
in
Mongolian

zehon
in
Amharic

zilonis
in
Latvian

zō
in
Japanese

To listen to native or fluent speakers
pronouncing words
that appear in this book,
please visit

levinequerido.com/AIsforBee

Words from the languages represented in this book can be found on these alphabet pages:

Afrikaans	Y		Hebrew	T		Navajo	N
Albanian	F, L		Hindi	B, S		Ojibwe	A, G
Alutiiq	I		Hungarian	R		Persian	R, X
Amharic	Z		Icelandic	M		Polish	O
Arabic	F, W		Igbo	A		Portuguese	A
Armenian	J		Indonesian	H		Quechua	P, U
Aymara	P		Irish	F		Russian	M
Azerbaijani	Q		Italian	F		Somali	W
Balinese	B		Japanese	N, T, Y, Z		Spanish	G
Basque	D, M		Javanese	I		Swahili	S
Chechen	E		Kannada	H		Swedish	M
Cherokee	D, E		Korean	G, N		Tagalog	I
Chichewa	C		Kurdish	R		Tamil	V
Czech	P		Latvian	Z		Telugu	C
Danish	R		Lithuanian	B		Thai	D, S
Estonian	J, K		Luxembourgish	D		Tlingit	X
Finnish	E, K		Malay	I		Turkish	A
French	E, L, R		Malayalam	S		Ukrainian	O
German	T		Mandarin	Q, X		Vietnamese	S
Greek	K		Māori	K		Wolof	W
Gujarati	U		Marathi	U		Yiddish	O
Hausa	B, J		Mongolian	Z		Zulu	I
Hawaiian	L		Nahuatl	C			

Author's Note

The words and languages in this book have been chosen for a variety of reasons, each of which has brought to light something I didn't know at the start of the project.

The featured animals are those that readers have probably seen before in alphabet books. Imagining translations of many different abecedaries all in one place, I tried to arrange familiar animals in an order that would be noticeably new. For example, in English, we are used to seeing *Z is for Zebra* on the final page. Rearranging the animals so that each would be represented by a handful of different-sounding translations that all begin with roughly the same sound or letter was a big puzzle and a lot of fun. In several languages, the spelling of a noun changes depending on whether it is definite or indefinite. In other languages, the commonly used English animal names were too general for direct translation. For example, in Tlingit, a language indigenous to the northwest coast of North America, where brown bears (*Ursus arctos*) and black bears (*Ursus americanus*) live, these two different species are not commonly grouped together but instead distinguished as *xóots* (brown bear) and *s'eek* (black bear). Similarly, in Nahuatl, a language spoken in Mexico and Central America, there is not a general word for all types of parrots, so *cochotl* refers to one of the most common in the area, the white-fronted parrot (*Amazona albifrons*). I've tried to reflect this in the illustrations.

When writing words in English, we use the Roman alphabet, which is also called the Latin alphabet. It represents different sounds with letters. Lots of languages use a version of the Roman alphabet. Because of this, if you can read in English you are able to sound out words in those other languages, such as Italian or Spanish. You may not know the meaning of the words you are reading, but you are still able to *say* them. However, many languages use their own unique writing systems. So, for English readers to be able to say words from these languages, the words must be *transliterated*. To transliterate is to take a word from a language with its own sounds and writing system and use the closest corresponding symbols or letters to write that word in a different writing system. This way, someone who does not know the language is still able to make the *sounds* of that word in that language. And of course, this is not always a simple task. For example, in Thai, the word for *turtle* is เต่า. At first, I did not know which sounds to make to say that word because I cannot speak or read Thai. So, I looked up the transliteration—in this case, the *Romanization*, which is transliteration from one language into the Roman alphabet. It turns out there are two different Romanizations of Thai. One of them spelled เต่า as *dtào* and the other as *tao*. The sounds *d* and *t* have a lot in common. In *phonetics*, which is the study of speech sounds, they're called *stops*, because for a moment all the air stops coming out of your mouth. In Thai, there are different stops than the *d* and *t* that we find in English. Some of them sound something in between. So, for this book, I picked *dtào*, because in this book *D is for Turtle*, but *T is for Octopus.*

Sometimes there are even MORE challenges! As a team, we set out to confirm each of these words with native speakers. But even then, different speakers of the same language can have different ideas about what the correct transliteration should be. What is the best Romanization of the Hebrew word for *octopus*? Is it *tmanun* or *tamnun*? Reasonable people will disagree, and it could start an interesting discussion about how language changes, or about the difference between consonants and vowels. In some cases, different dialects of a language use different words. For example, in Northern Kurdish, the word for *fox* is *rovî*, but in Central Kurdish, it is *rêwî*. In cases like this, we used the word that we were able to confirm with a native speaker. For consistency, when more than one word from a language is included in the book, we followed the style of one source. For example, both Cherokee words are transliterated following the SIYO Cherokee Language Engine, which also provides pronunciation recordings for each word.

Finally, the names of the languages represented in this book are written in English as they are commonly translated. For example, we use *French* instead of *Français*. These languages are currently spoken by a range of more than a billion speakers to a few hundred, and the 69 languages represented in this book are only a fraction of the more than 6,500 spoken across the world.

With gratitude to the Levine Querido team: Arthur Levine,
Meghan McCullough, Madelyn McZeal, Irene Vázquez, Nick Thomas, and
Antonio Gonzalez Cerna, and Andrea Wollitz at Recorded Books
for their enormous help in reaching out and connecting with friends, new
and old, who are native speakers of all these languages. And many thanks to
the speakers who shared their voices, words, and explanations. I learned
so much and wasn't even trying to translate a complete sentence!
Thank you.